The Great Piano Works of
JOHANN SEBASTIAN BACH

WARNER BROS. PUBLICATIONS - THE GLOBAL LEADER IN PRINT
USA: 15800 NW 48th Avenue, Miami, FL 33014

WARNER/CHAPPELL MUSIC

CANADA: 85 SCARSDALE ROAD, SUITE 101
DON MILLS, ONTARIO, M3B 2R2
SCANDINAVIA: P.O. BOX 533, VENDEVAGEN 85 B
S-182 15, DANDERYD, SWEDEN
AUSTRALIA: P.O. BOX 353
3 TALAVERA ROAD, NORTH RYDE N.S.W. 2113

NUOVA CARISCH

ITALY: VIA CAMPANIA, 12
20098 S. GIULIANO MILANESE (MI)
ZONA INDUSTRIALE SESTO ULTERIANO
SPAIN: MAGALLANES, 25
28015 MADRID
FRANCE: 25 RUE DE HAUTEVILLE, 75010 PARIS

INTERNATIONAL MUSIC PUBLICATIONS LIMITED

ENGLAND: SOUTHEND ROAD,
WOODFORD GREEN, ESSEX IG8 8HN
GERMANY: MARSTALLSTR. 8, D-80539 MUNCHEN
DENMARK: DANMUSIK, VOGNMAGERGADE 7
DK 1120 KOBENHAVNK

Project Manager: Dale Tucker
Design: Michael Ramsay

JOHANN SEBASTIAN BACH

Born: March 21, 1685-Eisenach, Germany
Died: July 28, 1750-Leipzig, Germany

Johann Sebastian Bach, the youngest of four children, was born on March 21, 1685 in Eisenach, Germany into a musical family which was active as performers, composers and teachers. In addition to his musical and academic studies, Bach's early training included Latin and Lutheranism at the Michaeliskirche in Lüneburg, where he was a chorister in the Mettenchor (boy choir). Here, he also accompanied the choir and performed on the violin. Although Bach took no formal lessons with an established composer, he learned from his family and studied works by both his contemporaries and predecessors. His initial compositional style was influenced by such keyboard masters as Froberger, Pachelbel, Frescobaldi, Buxtehude, and various French composers. Bach's keyboard fugal writing style was self-developed, and in this area he far exceeded that of other composers.

In 1707 Bach moved to Mülhausen where he wrote many church cantatas. During this year he married his first wife, Maria Barbara Bach, his cousin, who bore him seven children before her death in 1720. 1708 led Bach to the post of Konzertmeister (concert master) and court organist to the Duke of Weimar. During his stay in Weimar the majority of his organ works were composed. It is obvious, from the technical demands found in much of Bach's writing, that he was a gifted performer. In 1717 Bach moved to Cothen where the *Clavier-Büchlein,* unaccompanied violin works, and *Brandenburg Concertos* were composed. Anna Magdalena Wilcken became Bach's second wife in 1721, and later bore thirteen children.

Following the death of Johann Kuhnau, Bach applied for his post as cantor of Leipzig. As talented and respected as he was, Bach was given the position in 1723 only after it was declined by Telemann. Bach produced much of his choral music here, including the *St. John Passion, Mass in B Minor,* and the *Christmas Oratorio.* Other noted works from this period include the *Well-Tempered Clavier, Anna Magdalena Bach Notebook,* and the *Clavier-Übung.*

Often times, Bach built an entire large work around a single theme with his use of the canon, fugue, and counterpoint. He usually started with a sketch and built from there, involving numerous forms of a single idea. Left unfinished by his death, *The Art Of The Fugue* consists of double and triple fugues, interpolated canons, and a mirror fugue where Bach uses the subject forward and backward.

Following failing sight and health, Bach died on July 28, 1750, and is now buried at the Thomaskirche in Leipzig. He was one of the greatest contributors to the Baroque period with nearly 600 choral and vocal works, numerous orchestral and instrumental compositions, and over 400 keyboard works.

CONTENTS

Selected Pieces from "The Notebook for Anna Magdalena Bach"

Menuet in G Major 4
Menuet in G Minor 5
Menuet in G Major 6
Polonaise in G Minor 7
March in D Major 8
Musette in D Major 9
March in E Flat Major 10
March in G Major 12
Menuet in A Minor 13
Menuet in B Flat Major 14
Menuet in C Minor 15
Polonaise in G Minor 16
Menuet in F Major 17
Polonaise in G Major 18
Polonaise in G Minor 20
Polonaise in D Minor 22

Twelve Little Preludes

No. 1 23
No. 2 24
No. 3 24
No. 4 26
No. 5 27
No. 6 28
No. 7 28
No. 8 29
No. 9 30
No. 10 31
No. 11 32
No. 12 33

Jesu, Joy of Man's Desiring 34

Selected Two and Three Part Inventions

Invention No. 1 38
Invention No. 3 40
Invention No. 4 42
Invention No. 6 44
Invention No. 8 46
Invention No. 10 48
Invention No. 13 50
Sinfonia No. 1 52
Sinfonia No. 6 54
Sinfonia No. 8 56
Sinfonia No. 10 68
Sinfonia No. 11 60
Sinfonia No. 14 62

Selections from the French Suites

Two Minuets from Suite No. 1 64
Menuet from Suite No. 2 65
Anglaise from Suite No. 3 66
Sarabande from Suite No. 4 67
Air from Suite No. 4 68
Gavotte from Suite No. 5 69
Gavotte and Polonaise from Suite No. 5 70
Bourree from Suite No. 6 71

Selections from "Overture in the French Manner"

Gavotte No. 1 72
Gavotte No. 2 73
Passepied No. 1 74
Passepied No. 2 75
Sarabande 75
Bourree No. 1 76
Bourree No. 2 77

Selected Pieces from the Partitas

Corrente from Partita No. 1 78
Gigue from Partita No. 1 81
Menuet I from Partita No. 1 84
Menuet II from Partita No. 1 85
Sarabande from Partita No. 2 86
Rondeau from Partita No. 2 87
Capriccio from Partita No. 2 90
Fantasia from Partita No. 3 94
Gigue from Partita No. 3 98
Scherzo from Partita No. 3 100
Corrente from Partita No. 4 101
Prelude from Partita No. 5 103
Corrente from Partita No. 5 107
Air from Partita No. 6 109

Selected Preludes and Fugues from "The Well-Tempered Clavier"

Book I

Prelude No. 1 111
Prelude No. 2 114
Fugue No. 2 118
Prelude No. 5 121
Fugue No. 7 124
Prelude No. 10 128
Fugue No. 10 132
Prelude No. 15 135
Prelude No. 17 137
Prelude No. 20 140
Prelude No. 21 143

Book II

Fugue No. 1 146
Prelude No. 2 150
Prelude No. 5 152
Prelude No. 6 156
Fugue No. 6 159
Fugue No. 7 161
Fugue No. 9 164
Prelude No. 11 167
Prelude No. 12 172
Prelude No. 15 175
Fugue No. 15 178

Selections from the English Suites

Bourree from Suite No. 1 181
Gigue from Suite No. 2 182
Sarabande from Suite No. 5 184

Selected Pieces from
THE NOTEBOOK FOR ANNA MAGDALENA BACH
MENUET
in G Major

JOHANN SEBASTIAN BACH

MENUET
in G Minor

MENUET
in G Major

POLONAISE
in G Minor

MARCH
in D Major

MUSETTE
in D Major

MARCH
in E flat Major

MARCH
in G Major

MENUET
in A Minor

MENUET
in B♭ Major

MENUET
in C Minor

POLONAISE
in G Minor

MENUET
in F Major

POLONAISE
in G Major

POLONAISE
in G Minor

POLONAISE
in D Minor

TWELVE LITTLE PRELUDES

8.

Allegro. ($\dot{\bullet}$ = 116.)

JESU, JOY OF MAN DESIRING

Selected
TWO AND THREE PARTS INVENTIONS
INVENTION I

INVENTION III

INVENTION IV

INVENTION VI

INVENTION VIII

INVENTION X

INVENTION XIII

Allegro ♩ = 116

SINFONIA I

SINFONIA VI

SINFONIA VIII

SINFONIA X

SINFONIA XI

cresc. ma tranquillo

dim.

SINFONIA XIV

FRENCH SUITE NO. 1
in D Minor
TWO MINUETS

Moderato ♩ = 108

FRENCH SUITE NO. 2
in C Minor
MENUET

FRENCH SUITE NO. 3
in B Minor
ANGLAISE

FRENCH SUITE NO. 4
in E flat Major
SARABANDE

FRENCH SUITE NO. 4
in E flat Major
AIR

Moderato ♩ = 104

FRENCH SUITE NO. 5
in G Major
GAVOTTE

FRENCH SUITE NO. 6
in E Major
GAVOTTE and POLONAISE

FRENCH SUITE NO. 6
in E Major
BOURRÉE

Molto Allegro ♩ = 100

OVERTURE IN THE FRENCH MANNER

GAVOTTE I.

Allegro ♩ = 84

GAVOTTE II.

PASSEPIED I.

Allegro ♩ = 63

PASSEPIED II.

Passepied I da capo

SARABANDE
Andante con espressione ♩ = 72

BOURRÉE I.

Vivace ♩ = 96

BOURRÉE II.

PARTITA NO. 1
in B flat Major

CORRENTE
Vivace ♩ = 132

MENUET I

Allegro ♩. = 60

MENUET II

(la seconda volta **pp** *)*

PARTITA NO. 2
in C Minor

SARABANDE
Andante ♩ = 76
sempre espressivo

RONDEAU

Vivace ♩.= 84

p ben accentuato

90

CAPRICCIO
Allegro con brio ♩ = 126

PARTITA NO. 3
in A Minor

FANTASIA
Allegro ♩.= 69

GIGUE
Presto ♩. = 132
non troppo legato

mf   *ben accentuato*

SCHERZO
Allegro vivace ♩ = 126

PARTITA NO. 4
in D Major

CORRENTE
Allegro ♩ = 132

PARTITA NO. 5

in G Major

CORRENTE

PARTITA NO. 6
in E Minor

Selected Preludes and Fugues from

THE WELL-TEMPERED CLAVIER
Book I

PRAELUDIUM I.

(Moderato ♩ = 112)

PRAELUDIUM II.

(Allegro ♩ = 108)

energico

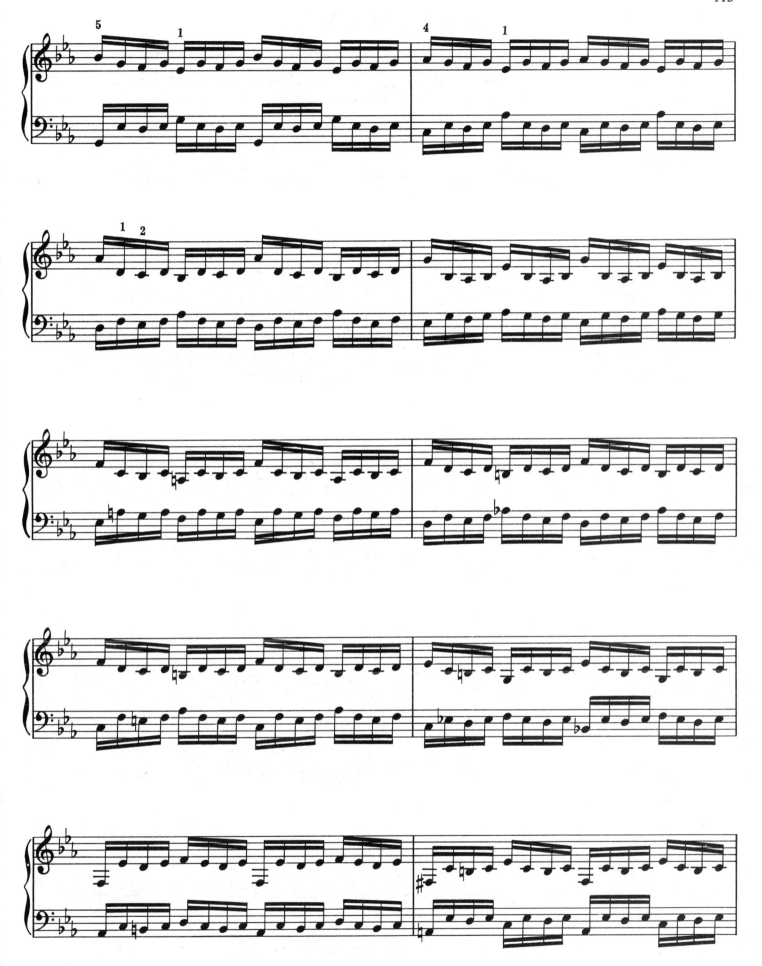

FUGA II.

PRAELUDIUM V.

FUGA VII.

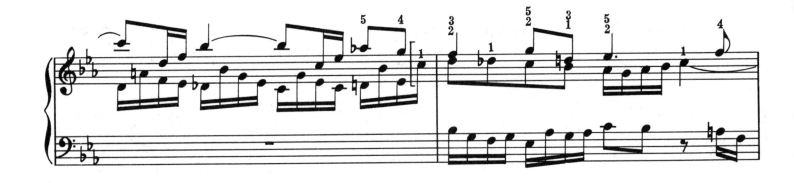

PRAELUDIUM X.

FUGA X.

PRAELUDIUM XV.

(Leggierissimo ♩.= 96)

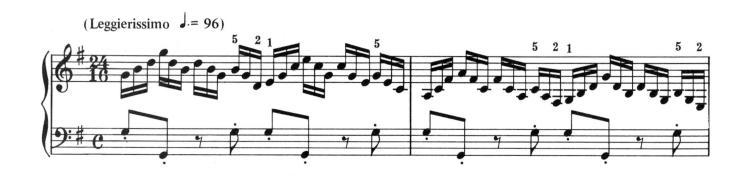

PRAELUDIUM XVII.

PRAELUDIUM XX.

PRAELUDIUM XXI.

144

Selected Preludes and Fugues from
THE WELL-TEMPERED CLAVIER
Book II
FUGA I.

PRAELUDIUM II.

Allegro spiritoso (♩ = 120)

sempre leggiermente staccato

PRAELUDIUM V.

Allegro (♩ ♩.= 84)

energico

PRAELUDIUM VI.

Allegro vivace (♩ = 120)

sempre staccato

FUGA VI.

Moderato (♩ = 72)

FUGA VII.

FUGA IX.

PRAELUDIUM XI.

Andante tranquillo (♩ = 60)

PRAELUDIUM XII.

Moderato (♩ = 80)

PRAELUDIUM XV.

Vivace (♩ = 132)

FUGA XV.

BOURRÉE NO. 2 IN A MINOR
(From English Suite No.1)

Allegretto

GIGUE IN A MINOR
(from English Suite No.2)

Vivace

SARABANDE
(from English Suite No.5)